The Blue-Eyed Monster
Dragged Me into Love

ROBERTO CARLOS MARTINEZ

PublishAmerica
Baltimore

First printing

At the specific preference of the author, PublishAmerica allowed this work to remain exactly as the author intended, verbatim, without editorial input.

ISBN: 1-4241-5832-X
PUBLISHED BY PUBLISHAMERICA, LLLP
www.publishamerica.com
Baltimore

Printed in the United States of America

To Mama Maria Erminia,

>*whose wisdom and strength prepared me for love.*

And my mother Maria Isabel,

>*the woman who gave birth to me and whose blood runs through my veins*

>*until I take my last breath.*

I

Your sexy intellect.
A type of mind bending exercise.
A moving pendulum that ceases to rust.

It captures me.
Into your world,
where the light blue flowers take light in and become red.
Drags me out of the hole that I am in.

It encircles me like a crowd witnessing a miracle,
elevates me like a tempestuous bull, and pushes me into that
serene place .
To limits I have never known.

It's you.
The kind of love that bends me and then turns me into sparkling
little pieces.

II

The other love left me.

That former love left me.

I shattered like a glass plate on concrete floor.
But I collected the pieces.
Dragging myself like a sloth, out of my misery.

Then you arrived.
With your translucent flame.
Filling in the cracks.
Filling me up with the mystery of love.

And I fell into blue eyes once more.
Drowning myself into the blueness that is you.

III

You, with the blue eyes.
Allow me to hide behind your perky smile.
I have a desire to admire you.
Trust the mirror and allow it to make two of you so that I can
love you more.

IV

"Let go," you said.
"I got you."

Memories ignited the journals,
for none had spoken such words.
In a silent world where I can never let go.
Clinging to the walls, not desiring to descend over the ledge.
Gasping for air like a fish in an empty bowl.

"Let go," you said.
"I got you."

I never let go until you.

Concealed, frail emotions.
Walls that had enclosed me like land around water.

Then I let go.
And I felt like hell had frozen over.

V

You dwell in others, my love.
And I surrender to love with them
like I did with you.

VI

Pardon yourself my love.
Pardon yourself when you hurt me.

When you place me against the walls.
The sharp needles, cold stones, and aroused fires.

And after the hurt is over, I still love you.

VII

Unfortunately you're taken.
But if you yearned for me, I don't think I could resist.

I do not know.
I do not know.

For I would lose all sense of reason.
And my flesh would be like the river that flows back into the sea.

VIII

I've known you before.
In a distant place.
An abyss, perhaps a diminished memory.

Yet the memories.
They stir like bubbles in red-hot lava.

I've known you before.
I've savored those lips.
I've gazed into those gorgeous blue eyes.
I've felt that body close to mine.
In some other time, I let that consume me.

I still savor sweetness.
The delicate taste of you.

IX

Once you came along.
I lost command.
I let the emotions absorb me.
Bending me, folding every part of me into an envelope.

I couldn't gaze at the sky during the daytime.
You existed there, your blue eyes.
Hands, I could not touch, for they held memories of you.

When I was lost, I saw you.

X

Your mentality.
It astonishes me.
Driving me into madness like a woman who has lost her child.

Numbers, words, they confuse me.
Mistaken smiles, mystical glances, they make me nervous.

For I do not know if you love me.

But I want you.
Grasp me violently while I smile and relish the ride.
Let me experience your delicate fresh lips claiming me.

Then the road would open, enveloping me into you.

XI

Three white doves landed on my hand.
Twenty serpents crept into my heart.
But my soul chose to take flight.

I confess.
I don't know if I have revealed this to you.
But I don't have any recollections of love.
Affection, embraces, kisses they do not exist here.
Only malicious words provided that.

Hollow walls have failed to speak.
Hands.
Only there to cause pain.
Words, electric wires marking my boundaries.
Lips I never did feel, for I could only admire their beauty.

To say I love you, when no one ever spoke those words to me
would be clinging to death itself.
Those who recited those words to me, lied.

For love is reliable and harmonious.
It's a creature in nature.
It walks into fresh roads,
clings on to the things it needs,
and it attends to the safety of others.

XII

My aggressive love.
Determined like the energetic bald eagle.
A beast, set free.
Eager to fight like the bull.
My blue-eyed love, color the sky for me and paint the sea.

On certain occasions we fight.
We construct the sounds of the most furious Rap music.
But the make up sex is the finest.
It lays us to rest like peace after war.
My silent love you crawl into me.
My fortunate love, you expose the angelic smile in me.

XIII

Let it go love,
release the anger!
Don't give in to the emotion.
Don't give me that look of a possum dangling from a tree!

I still love you!
Even after you preferred another.
I still love you!
I've never witnessed someone choose shit over water!

I still love you!
After you deserted me.
I still love you!
After you emptied me out of a glass container.
I still love you!
After you abandoned me like a bag of marijuana on a table for all
to share.

I still love you!
Even after you said you obtained some other one.

"We can just have fun," you said.

XIV

If you became sugar and I honey,
maybe things would be different.

If time was a mortal, you would do the same.
You would drag my love, filling it with filth.
Then you would toss it into the sea.

XV

I am a little crazy.
I think of you, like a madman next to the sea.
Anticipating your return.

Allowing the wind to run around every region of my body.
The sounds of the waves, tumbling into my ears.
Time ticking violently, only to accomplish its end.

Love perishes,
but it leaves behind filth.

XVI

Love suddenly takes grasp of you, taking your breath away.
Losing your sense of control.
Tightens itself on you, making you powerless like a piece of
paper in the fire.

You assume its shape.
Once it has slowly let go,
you lie there, confused like a rat a serpent has released.

XVII

The first time I fixed my eyes on your blue eyes.
My mind carried me to that place.
Deep down in my heart.

The red core I set to black.
The spider webs, they take it's shape.
Twisting, molding into the unknown.

A place I resist to open.

XVIII

Get close.
Get as close as you want to be.
Don't limit yourself.
Be like the bird who flies with the wind.
Capture me with your grace.

XIX

You remind me so much of the other one.
The one who rocked the earth with excitement.
Filled the sea with clear spring water.
The tender look like a baby looking at a teddy bear.
The quick smile, the ocean colored eyes.
The sultry walk, like honey over French toast.

XX

Unspoken words that feel like meal worms in my mind.

The kisses I failed to give.

I was a feather caught in a tornado.
A rose filled with vibrant colors,
expecting to collapse in its own weight.
A fountain wasting water.

With your loss, I gained myself.

XXI

My love.

My crush.

The one I fantasize about.
Who fills me like a bottle of champagne.

A future for us.
More real than a daydream, as pleasant as a day of rest.

Making things up in my heart.
Every little piece of you fading into my eyes.

Empty-headed me.
You haven't even mentioned a word of love to me.

XXII

I look into your blue eyes and I can't find my voice.
Lost in a distant sea.

Your eyes speak, but your lips do not move.

I cannot say, I cannot say.
You just stand there as you see me walk away.

XXIII

The sweetest love.
A natural, soothing flavor like Asian green tea.
The loveliest phrase.

Words drain into my heart.

When I walk around you, I see the light.
The lighting on a picture.
The color on a flower.

With you, yellow turns to red and I let myself go.

XXIV

An exotic fear takes me over.
I turn to debris and begin to shiver.

Fear,
when I get close to you.
It's a battlefield for me, defending myself against sweet desire.
To want to experience your touch, and surrender to the feeling.

When you come, I wrap myself around you like a serpent.

XXV

Damn!
I love you!
No matter how many times I think about it.

Our lips coming together.
Creating the sound of a romantic violin.

Your blue, nut shaped eyes take me away to the sea.

Where I forget, where I forgive.

XXVI

Many times I have perished in the arms of another.
Consumed in whiteness,
frightened.
The light runs out of my round eyes like ants out of an ant hole
filled with smoke.

When my soul returns,
I do not know how it works.

I allow the sea to surround me, claiming me from all sides.
I become a freckle on a body.

The sea carries me away into serenity.
To the richest emotion.
To the most restful song.

XXVII

Beware.
Beware of the apple that descends from the neighboring tree.
Encage it and throw it out to sea before it creeps up on you.

Allow it to sleep.
Allow it to sleep.
The savage beast, acquiring those it can pull in.
An open tomb.

Allow the creature of flesh to sleep.
Then it will come to pass because it has lost power.

XXVIII

You, my single love,
concealed love.
I dwell in you.

I hide in my shell, a turtle, shielding myself from you.
Attempts to go against the wind are futile,
it profoundly crawls into every pore of my body.

But I fight the stillness of the earth.

To refuse this love is to refuse my essence.
You're my mellow days, my fruitful smiles, my innocent
desires.
Time causes me to love you more.
I give in to you like a vine climbing along the surrounding walls.
I let your wave consume me, and I adorn myself in it.

XXIX

Your sweet, adoring lips.
Your eagle eyes,
gazing at me with your keen sight.
The awareness of your intense eyes,
taking me piece by piece, making me your own.

Seeking you like the sweetest passion fruit.
Sampling you like an enigmatic taste.
Holding onto you like my life depends on it.

You take the timid me like a rainbow after the storm.
I let the rain come down on me and we become the sea.

XXX

Sweet words.
Don't use them on me.
It's dreadful, to allow them to enter my ears to the beat of drums.

Grasp my delicate hands and caress them.
Feel my desolation.
The desolation that claims every pattern in me.

Secure your eyes on me as I cede to you.
I let your gaze take control.

Shelter me from the world.
Possess me like a tree possesses a branch.
Never release me.

XXXI

Your quiet lips, your tender blue eyes, your dripping wet hair.
They drive me crazy.
An illusion, a kind of misconception.
Your firm chest, saturated skin, and impeccable face.

They demand me.
I thirst, I crave.

Your intense legs, your virtuous back, your everything else.
I want it, I crave it, I take it.

XXXII

Trust your lips.
Let them search for mine like a hot day searching for water.
Your eyes see each and every part of me.
Your hands seek what you desire.

Merge your body with mine.
Two ice cubes consuming each other.

Indulge in love.
Feed your desire.
Give in to me.

XXXIII

Undress me.
Look for what belongs to you.

I am yours.
Lick me like the most invigorating drop of water.
Bite me passionately as biting into the most savory piece of mango.

Take what's yours.

Stir me into you, shake me to your rhythm.
The juices mix and our lips seal together.

Let's make a cocktail, perhaps a margarita.
Afterwards, we'll want more.

XXXIV

When you kiss my neck, I start to stir.
You make your way around.
Discovering the path in.

Then you open the cage and release the beast within me.
The untamed dog waiting to be taken by a thunderous passion.

Then we prepare for the ride.
Driving each other into inclination.
Creating our own rhythms.
Raging drums, persuasive violins, and clicking maracas.

XXXV

With you I forget everything.
I fade at the sight of your blue eyes.
My mind goes into a blank state.
A bubble I refuse to shatter.

I melt into your arms.
Ice cream, honey, a mix of cinnamon and milk.

You're the most sparkling wine.
The fresh taste in life.
I bend, I twist onto you.

It's only when reality regenerates that I feel imperfect.
I become a glass of water shaking in an earthquake.
It is then I notice my decorative wrinkles and my fading skin color.

XXXVI

Love.

Love...If only I could hide beneath it.
Beneath the torrid taste of your lips.
Allowing your eyes to surround me.
And your hands to take me over,
surrendering myself like a river into an ocean.

When it's over,
I take a piece of you like a pearl on a necklace.

XXXVII

I saw you get within me.
You, the one who looked as young as a mare.
A dark whisper in the wind.
I see your roots, follicles wedged into every piece of me.
Multiplying, sticking, occupying me.

I dedicated myself to you.

Your deep wings took me.
Fading me into white, black and orange colors.

A time so advanced.
Of this I did not know.

You, the one who reminded me of a teddy bear.
But when we made love you seemed so aged.
A painting that ages the closer you get to it.

You, my love.
The one who opened my eyes like seashells waiting to be filled.
The one who opened my eyes to what I had simply heard of.

You.
I call you.
I crave you, an ageless obsession.
The silence speaks to me.
Seated here, seated here.

Ready, waiting to discover your song once again.

XXXVIII

I remember…

You left me
there in the corner,
breathing loneliness.

XXXIX

Love arrives like a sparkling sea bubble lifted by the wind.
Claimed by every pore of that lifeless body hanging from
rusted chains.
Releasing you from what was once called reality.

Sepals and petals begin to grow from the heart.
Once it's fleshy, the heart beats to the emotion that has
awakened within.

Misty particles fill the eyes.
The body begins to move to the sound of an enchanting flute.

You feel the ticking in your brain.
Time has awakened the rest of you.

One day you experience the dust at your toes once more.
Water has run out of you like fish left dangling in Summer sun.

But once the body knows love, it does not forget.
Memories run through cells like drops of water in an extremely hot
frying pan.

XL

You're my moonlight shaded in green.
With a taste of blue and a glimpse of red.

You're luminous smile conceals my reality.

Allow your charisma to speak to me and your sexuality to awaken me.

A combination of your love and your desire would make my intellect fail.

XLI

There's sugariness in your silence.
A sense of taste I take from you.

Your voice, I follow it.
Searching its origin.

I take you in
and I smile.
You say nothing.
But I feel everything.

It's that silent love,
speaking to me in unknown tongues.

I awaken to your silence.
I see into your smile.

XLII

You're so cute when you make mistakes.
Adorable as a child who repeats "I love you."
That smile that runs over you like sand into the sea.
That glitter in your eyes.
It only makes me love you more.

It's the strength in your insecurities.
Your victory in times of failure.

Your smile alone makes up for your mistakes.

XLIII

Following your tracks through the windy desert
I realize I miss you.

That your voice will no longer awaken these ears.
That your eyes will no longer cause me to daydream.
That your seaworthy lips I will no longer taste.
That your smile will no longer set me to sleep.

You will no longer stir the silence in me.

I guess it wasn't meant to be.
You take the river.
And I take the sea.

XLIV

I miss you, my blue-eyed one.
Time doesn't let go of you.
The memories create an image of you in my head.
My senses begin to react.
They add your sweet soft lips and your cool calming breath.

Why I let you go, I do not know.
The absence of sitting beside you.
The tender warmth of your hands on my cheeks.
To glance into your eyes was a glimpse into happiness.

I question whether you still think of me.
I dread witnessing you once more.
Fearful of looking frail and absurd.

There are times when I need you.

The feeling of adventure, swimming though the deep oceans of
immortality.

XLV

Today I was hurting, my love.
The hurt had reached my heart.
And the red veins had released it.

At that instant I thought of you.
I thought how wonderful it would be.
For you to be there, holding my hand.
To let me know all things will pass.

I closed my eyelids,
clenched my hands until I saw white.
In the whiteness I wished to see you again.
To tolerate your blue eyes watching over me.
Feeling your presence like an angel
who lends peace into my soul.

XLVI

My body shakes and shudders.
Why do you scare me?
My eyes look away.
But they fight, they fight to look once more.

Afraid to say I love you.
My eyes start to fade into blue.

XLVII

You turn your head to the side.
So that I may kiss you.
I lay next to you.
Waiting for more.

XLVIII

When the breath of love has once lived in you,
you tend to go back.
To the silent well where nothing weighed.

Where time had ceased like the ticking of a clock.

Only your lips moved like a drop of rain over a leaf.
That hidden place under the solemn stars.
Whispering through the passive trees.
Lost under the rainforest of love.

When the breath of love has once lived in you,
you tend to go back.

Those memories bring to your lips a syrupy taste of molasses.

XLIX

I wonder what you are concealing behind those peculiar blue
eyes.
They come alive under the moonlight.
In the dark, they silently sit in their sockets.

The quality of your lovers.
The number of lies you have told.
The two sides of a mirror.

When I kiss you, I sense the unusual one.
The one who exists deep inside, awaiting release.

L

Half of you would simply disgust me.
All of you would be sweet.
That sweetness would cause my senses to come alive.

In my mind, I will always have all of you.
Your voice that bounced against the walls of my inner ear.
Your beauty that left an imprint in my eyes.

The choices you made are just another component of you.

I wonder if I would choose you again.

If you return, will you declare your love to me?

Perhaps to be with you would cause me to feel filthy,
to know who you had been with.
I would wonder whether that love was superb
or if that person was silently swimming through your mind
when we made love.

LI

Don't get mad my love.
Take a deep breath out of your fragile box.
It's a different environment.
You're not in control.

Just relax.

"It doesn't matter."
"It's no longer you're universe."

LII

Counting is not easy.
To count the kisses you gave me.
To count the times I let the earth sit still for you.

I can only count the times I have loved you.
That's once.
Once.

LIII

You stepped through the door of my life and I let that breeze
consume me.
I fell into the journey of your admirable blue eyes.
Feelings of fear and excitement dissolved my loneliness.

I faithfully fell into the loneliness of your lips.
Where life had formerly flourished, with beauty of a million roses.

I was taken deep inside you, where kisses turned into nothingness.
Where colors captured my eyes and turned them into soft glass.

One day I came to terms with this beauteous paradox.
Breaking through the glass webs I felt the strength in me once again.

LIV

Words unfold today.
Silence awakens and lives.
Me, alive again.